DRINKS
FOR MUNDANE TASKS

Created, published, and distributed by Knock Knock
1635 Electric Ave.
Venice, CA 90291
knockknockstuff.com
Knock Knock is a registered trademark of Knock Knock LLC

Illustrations by Fausto Montanari

This book is a work of humor and meant solely for entertainment
purposes and for responsible adults of legal drinking age in their
respective country and/or state and/or province. You should never
operate machinery or try to actually perform tasks, mundane or
otherwise, while drinking. In no event will Knock Knock be liable
to any reader for any harm, injury, or damages, including direct,
indirect, incidental, special, consequential, or punitive arising out
of or in connection with the use of the information contained in this
book. So there.

ISBN: 978-168349006-7
UPC: 825703-50174-2

10 9 8 7 6 5 4 3

DRINKS ~FOR~ MUNDANE TASKS

SEVENTY COCKTAIL RECIPES FOR EVERYDAY CHORES
FROM DOING THE DISHES TO REFILLING THE STAPLER TO CALLING MOM

DAVID VIENNA

KNOCK KNOCK®
VENICE, CALIFORNIA

CONTENTS

Dinner parties, art-show premieres, date night—special events seem to get all the cocktails. Indeed, rare moments are celebrated and most celebrations call for drinks. Perhaps that's just because of a lack of vision—a limit to the scope within which people choose to view everyday duties. Should brushing your teeth be any less of a cause for celebration than winning an award? No. Clearly, the people who claim otherwise have not seen your winning smile. Within the pages of this book, you'll find unique artisan cocktail pairings for the things real people do every day, thus proving it is not the event that makes the cocktail worthy, but rather the cocktail that makes the task an event.

When enjoying a task/cocktail pairing, it is recommended that you prepare the corresponding libation before attempting the work. After all, the book is called *Drinks for Mundane Tasks*, not *Drinks for After You've Completed Mundane Tasks*. It is also recommended that you adjust the recipes as needed. If scraping a lime peel for some zest proves difficult after your second drink, it's okay if you just squeeze some lime juice into the mix instead. You'll need to save what's left of your motor functions for whatever task you're doing anyway.

On the topic of recommendations, books such as these would typically use this space to provide a list of tips, tools, and techniques to prepare you so thoroughly for the job of making fancy drinks that you could open your own downtown nightclub. This book, however, will make no such suggestions. Your home is a judgment-free zone. If you only have the bottom-shelf rum, go ahead and use it. If you don't have a three-inch dual-blade garnish peeler, don't feel blue, just pull the butter knife out of the silverware drawer. If you're out of martini glasses, go ahead and use your kid's plastic Batman cup, a mason jar, a goldfish bowl—it's fine. See? *Judgment-free zone.* Unless you have to flush a goldfish to use the goldfish bowl. Then, perhaps you should reconsider.

Besides, it can be said with a fair degree of certainty that the only people who have a bar completely stocked with every single tool or liquor you'd ever need are mixologists. And that word was invented by these same people to justify their annoying perfectionism.

This book *does* offer more than just recipes for yummy cocktails, though. There are also:

- » Informative sidebars (not to give too much away, but Aztec gods are mentioned)

- » Recipe variations (twists on recipes for similar tasks because, let's be honest, clipping fingernails and clipping toenails are *not* the same thing)

- » An alcohol index (if you want to skip the handy categories and go straight to your favorite booze)

- » A durable cover that makes a fantastic garnish cutting board in a pinch

Enjoy the book and, as they say, drink responsibly. Of course, since you're doing tasks around the house, you're already responsible. So, just drink.

Bottoms up.

CHAPTER ONE

KITC

SINI

HEN
KING

DOING
THE DISHES

The cups, bowls, and plates from breakfast are stacked so high, they create a magnificent skyline of glass and ceramic, speckled with hardened oatmeal and dried orange pulp. Someone needs to clean up this metropolis, and the spongy mantle has fallen to you. The powerful blue hue of liquid soap, the Dishwater is your faithful sidekick...minus the grappling hook.

THE DISHWATER

INGREDIENTS

2 OZ SPICED RUM
½ OZ MIDORI
½ OZ CURAÇAO
½ OZ LEMON JUICE
7UP

INSTRUCTIONS

COMBINE RUM, MIDORI, CURAÇAO, AND LEMON JUICE IN A SHAKER WITH ICE. SHAKE, THEN STRAIN INTO AN OLD FASHIONED GLASS. TOP OFF WITH 7UP. (NOTE: IF YOUR OLD FASHIONED GLASSES ARE ALL DIRTY, USE WHATEVER GLASS IS CLEAN, OR YOU MAY SIMPLY DRINK THE RUM FROM THE BOTTLE AND CHASE WITH 7UP.)

BEVERAGE COMPANIES INFUSE VODKA WITH EVERYTHING FROM FRUIT TO BACON. BUT INFUSING VODKA IS MUCH EASIER THAN YOU MIGHT THINK. (AT LEAST FOR FRUIT—BACON MIGHT BE HARDER.) JUST CHOP UP THE CHOSEN FRUIT AND USE A 1-TO-1 RATIO: 3 CUPS OF CHOPPED FIGS, FOR EXAMPLE, CAN BE MIXED WITH 3 CUPS OF VODKA. GET AN AIRTIGHT CONTAINER BIG ENOUGH FOR YOUR CONCOCTION. PUT THE FRUIT IN THE CONTAINER, THEN THE VODKA. IF ANY FRUIT REMAINS EXPOSED, POUR IN MORE VODKA TO MAKE SURE IT'S COVERED. SEAL IT UP AND LEAVE IT FOR ABOUT FIVE DAYS. GIVE IT A SHAKE EVERY DAY OR TWO. THEN, STRAIN IT INTO ANOTHER CONTAINER AND ENJOY. AND ENJOY AND ENJOY AND ENJOY.

WIPING DOWN
THE KITCHEN COUNTER

The epic meal you prepared for your friends was a hoot to make, but now the kitchen counter looks like the scene of some sort of battle. Clear everything off and get ready to wipe it down. While you're spraying antibacterial cleanser hither and yon, keep one hand free for your own antibacterial solution—the Formula 410. Though not a typical choice, the delicious drink could be considered a digestif solely because by the time you're enjoying it, you've already eaten.

THE FORMULA 410

INGREDIENTS

2 OZ LEMON-INFUSED
  VODKA
1½ TSP WHITE CURAÇAO
1 TSP BRANDY
1 TSP LIME JUICE
LEMON

INSTRUCTIONS

MIX VODKA, CURAÇAO, BRANDY, AND LIME JUICE IN A COCKTAIL SHAKER WITH ICE. STRAIN INTO COCKTAIL GLASS, GARNISH WITH A WEDGE OF LEMON. DON'T LET THE FACT YOUR KITCHEN AND YOUR COCKTAIL BOTH SMELL LEMON-FRESH THROW YOU.

UNPACKING
GROCERIES

When returning from the market, things are never as simple as just putting groceries where they go. There are expiration dates to check, pantry shelves to reorganize, and some kind of weird stain in the fridge produce drawer. Before you get started, mix yourself a Brown Bag. It's like a coupon for your tired soul. Plus, the garnish will help clear space for the new fruit you just bought.

THE BROWN BAG

INGREDIENTS

2 OZ WHISKEY
1 OZ DRAMBUIE
½ OZ LEMON JUICE
½ OZ PINEAPPLE JUICE
LEMON
PINEAPPLE

INSTRUCTIONS

COMBINE WHISKEY, DRAMBUIE, LEMON JUICE, AND PINEAPPLE JUICE IN A BLENDER WITH ICE. BLEND AND POUR INTO AN OLD FASHIONED GLASS. GARNISH WITH LEMON AND PINEAPPLE SLICES. IF ANY OF THE INGREDIENTS ARE AT THE BOTTOM OF A GROCERY BAG, UNPACK THAT ONE FIRST.

DECIDING
WHAT'S FOR DINNER

The eternal debate over whether to have chicken, fish, pasta, or a big salad often goes on so long, all parties end up just eating saltines out of the box over the sink and wondering where the night went wrong. Relax with a Leftover, which will inspire you to, at the very least, land on an entrée or, at worst, attempt that fancy bacon-potato-muffin recipe you saw on an Internet video.

THE LEFTOVER

INGREDIENTS

2 OZ VODKA
1 OZ CRÈME DE CACAO
LIME

INSTRUCTIONS

MIX VODKA AND CRÈME DE CACAO IN A COCKTAIL SHAKER WITH ICE. STRAIN INTO A COCKTAIL GLASS AND SQUEEZE LIME WEDGE INTO DRINK. COUNT THE DRINK CALORIES TOWARD YOUR MEAL.

ORDERING
PIZZA DELIVERY

The drawer that holds all of the delivery menus and coupons also holds old charging cords, coins, empty pens, and, for some reason, a stack of old photos from your office Christmas party three years ago. (When you decide to clean out this drawer, try a Coins and Markers, pg. 24.) And after digging them out, it looks like all of the coupons are expired. Plus, no one can decide on whether they want a cheese with black olives or a pepperoni with mushrooms. Ordering a pizza should not be this difficult. An Italian Job gives you the calming sensation of sitting at an outdoor café in Florence. Si beve, si è soddisfatti.

THE ITALIAN JOB

INGREDIENTS

2 OZ GIN
1 OZ CAMPARI
½ OZ SAUVIGNON BLANC
ORANGE
PEPPERONI

INSTRUCTIONS

MIX GIN, CAMPARI, AND WINE IN A COCKTAIL SHAKER WITH ICE. STRAIN INTO AN OLD FASHIONED GLASS FULL OF ICE. GARNISH WITH A TWIST OF ORANGE AND A SLICE OF PEPPERONI.

WAITING
FOR PASTA WATER TO BOIL

The water in the pot on the stove doesn't care that your stomach is screaming for dinner. It only cares about physics and perhaps some thermodynamics. You know this because it's taking forever to boil while you stare impotently at a box of whole-wheat spaghetti. Since you have some time, mix up a Watched Pot. The sangria-like mix of fruit and wine (with a kick of rum) should give you the strength to fight the urge to simply pour yourself a bowl of cereal and go to bed.

THE WATCHED POT

INGREDIENTS

2 OZ RUM
1 OZ SAUVIGNON BLANC
1 OZ LEMON JUICE
1 OZ ORANGE JUICE
1 TSP SIMPLE SYRUP
SYRAH
LEMON
DRY SPAGHETTI

INSTRUCTIONS

MIX RUM, WINE, LEMON JUICE, ORANGE JUICE, AND SIMPLE SYRUP IN A MIXING GLASS. POUR INTO A HIGHBALL GLASS FILLED WITH ICE AND THEN TOP OFF WITH SYRAH. GARNISH WITH A LEMON WEDGE AND A FEW DRY SPAGHETTI NOODLES. HOPEFULLY, BY THE TIME THE NOODLES ARE LIMP, THE WATER WILL BE READY.

WHILE WAITING FOR THE BUBBLES TO APPEAR IN THE WATER LETTING YOU KNOW THE WATER IS BOILING, HOW ABOUT SOME INTERESTING INFO ABOUT ANOTHER BUBBLY LIQUID? CHAMPAGNE HAS HELPED CLASSY PEOPLE GET SCHNOCKERED FOR CENTURIES, AND THAT CORK POP ALWAYS ANNOUNCES A CELEBRATION. BUT, HOW FAST WOULD THAT CORK TRAVEL IF YOU JUST LET IT FLY? WHILE THE ANSWER VARIES DEPENDING ON FACTORS SUCH AS TEMPERATURE AND SIZE OF THE BOTTLE, THE GENERAL ANSWER IS BETWEEN TWENTY-FIVE AND FORTY MILES PER HOUR. THAT ALONE IS A PRETTY GOOD REASON TO KEEP A GRIP ON IT OR, AT LEAST, POINT THE BOTTLE AT A VASE YOU DON'T LIKE.

MAKING
SCHOOL LUNCHES

Crusts? Gone. Jelly? Not too much. Peanut butter? On both slices to prevent sogginess. There is no greater master of the PB&J sandwich than you. Add a snack bag of chips for fun and a few baby carrots to make the whole thing moderately nutritious. Boom! Done. Celebrate with the Liquid Lunch. With its egg white protein and peach, it's about as healthy as the lunch you just made.

THE LIQUID LUNCH

INGREDIENTS

2 OZ BOURBON
1 OZ LIME JUICE
½ OZ SIMPLE SYRUP
1 TSP PEACH PRESERVES
1 EGG WHITE
PEACH

INSTRUCTIONS

MIX BOURBON, LIME JUICE, SIMPLE SYRUP, PEACH PRESERVES, AND EGG WHITE IN A COCKTAIL SHAKER WITH ICE. STRAIN INTO A CHILLED OLD FASHIONED GLASS. GARNISH WITH A SLICE OF PEACH AND SERVE WITH THE CUT CRUSTS OF THE PB&J.

MAKING
YOUR KID'S BREAKFAST

The dreams of preparing a table full of delicious pancakes, eggs over easy, bacon, biscuits, and fruit picked fresh from your garden have devolved to handing over a slice of cold cheese pizza while your child watches Saturday morning cartoons. Never fear. The Liquid Omelet offers a complete breakfast in a glass—fruit, eggs, bacon, and just enough bourbon to inspire a mid-morning nap.

THE LIQUID OMELET

INGREDIENTS

2 OZ BOURBON
1 OZ LIME JUICE
½ OZ SIMPLE SYRUP
1 TSP PEACH PRESERVES
1 EGG WHITE
BACON

INSTRUCTIONS

MIX BOURBON, LIME JUICE, SIMPLE SYRUP, PEACH PRESERVES, AND EGG WHITE IN A COCKTAIL SHAKER WITH ICE. STRAIN INTO A CHILLED OLD FASHIONED GLASS. GARNISH WITH A PIECE OF COOKED BACON. IF TRAINING FOR A BOXING MATCH, SERVE WITH THE EGG YOLK IN A SHOT GLASS.

SORTING
ITEMS IN THE JUNK DRAWER

The junk drawer in your home holds every piece of flotsam and jetsam randomly acquired—from empty ballpoint pens to bent paper clips to a key that unlocks the door of the apartment in which you lived four years prior. When you can stuff no more loose batteries or drill bits into it, let the bubbly Coins and Markers make organizing the drawer a joyous affair.

THE COINS AND MARKERS

INGREDIENTS

HEFEWEIZEN
7UP

INSTRUCTIONS

SIMULTANEOUSLY POUR HEFEWEIZEN AND 7UP INTO A CHILLED PINT GLASS. COLLECT ALL THE FRANCS, DUCALS, AND OTHER PRE-EURO FOREIGN CURRENCY AT THE BACK OF THE DRAWER TO USE AS REPLACEMENT BOARD GAME PIECES.

BED,
AND BO

BATH,
RING

VACUUMING

As a cleaning device, the vacuum disappoints. Once a room is vacuumed, it just needs to be vacuumed again in a week or so. You might as well be vacuuming a boulder up a hill. Right? The hearty This Sucks, a spin on the classic Bloody Mary, makes you okay with the fact that the clump of old dog hair won't come up from the living room rug. Use the vacuum crevice tool to see if you can pick up the pieces of your broken life.

THIS SUCKS

INGREDIENTS

2 CLOVES GARLIC
3 OZ BEEF STOCK
3 OZ TOMATO JUICE
½ OZ LIME JUICE
3 DASHES TABASCO
    SAUCE
3 DASHES
    WORCESTERSHIRE
2 OZ TEQUILA
GROUND PEPPER

INSTRUCTIONS

MINCE GARLIC CLOVES. COMBINE BEEF STOCK, TOMATO JUICE, LIME JUICE, TABASCO, WORCESTERSHIRE, AND GARLIC IN A SAUCE-PAN AND STIR OVER LOW HEAT. (DO NOT BOIL.) POUR TEQUILA INTO A COFFEE MUG, FOLLOWED BY THE HEATED MIXTURE. ADD PEPPER TO TASTE. DRINK ONE PER ROOM UNTIL THE FLOOR IS CLEAN OR YOU'RE PASSED OUT ON IT.

DUSTING

The ads for those new dust wipes promise to make the job not just easy, but downright magical. Did you see the way they just effortlessly lift the dust from that oak table? It was like a sorcerer's spell. So, you picked up a box at the store and you're itching to give them a try. First, you've got your own magic to do—a potion called This Blows, an Asian twist on the Bloody Mary that's sure to clear the dust from your mind while you clear the dust from the armoire.

THIS BLOWS

INGREDIENTS

2 CLOVES GARLIC
3 OZ VEGETABLE STOCK
3 OZ TOMATO JUICE
½ OZ LIME JUICE
3 DASHES
  WORCESTERSHIRE
2 OZ SAKE
1 PINCH FRESHLY
  GRATED WASABI
GROUND PEPPER

INSTRUCTIONS

MINCE GARLIC CLOVES. COMBINE VEGETABLE STOCK, TOMATO JUICE, LIME JUICE, WORCESTERSHIRE, AND GARLIC IN A SAUCE PAN AND STIR OVER LOW HEAT. (DO NOT BOIL.) POUR SAKE INTO A COFFEE MUG, FOLLOWED BY THE HEATED MIXTURE. STIR IN WASABI, AND ADD PEPPER AND DUST PARTICLES TO TASTE.

DOING
LAUNDRY

Wash, dry, fold, stack, repeat. The janitor cleaning the gym locker room doesn't see this much underwear. And where did all those single socks go? The pile of freshly washed and dried clothes may put a wrinkle in your day, but thanks to the apricot garnish of the Lost Sock, you'll get plenty of iron. Now, the steps are wash, dry, fold, stack, *sip*, repeat.

THE LOST SOCK

INGREDIENTS

2 OZ RYE
1 OZ DRY VERMOUTH
1 DASH ANGOSTURA
  BITTERS
APRICOT

INSTRUCTIONS

MIX RYE, VERMOUTH, AND BITTERS IN A COCKTAIL SHAKER WITH ICE. SHAKE, STRAIN INTO A MARTINI GLASS, AND GARNISH WITH APRICOT. CONSIDER LEAVING THE LAUNDRY UNTIL TOMORROW.

IRONING

Do artists ever iron their clothes? Probably not. Do carefree kids or old-timey transients? No. Sadly, your office does have a dress code and the bosses might look down on anyone wearing something that looked like it was just pulled from the wastebasket. So, you've got the ironing board all ready, the iron is hot, you're just missing one thing—the warming elixir called the Hard Pressed. It will remove all the creases from your soul.

THE HARD PRESSED

INGREDIENTS

2 OZ SPICED RUM
6 OZ HARD APPLE CIDER
1 TSP HONEY
4 CLOVES
NUTMEG

INSTRUCTIONS

COMBINE RUM, CIDER, HONEY, AND CLOVES IN A SAUCEPAN OVER MEDIUM HEAT. STIR UNTIL MIXTURE IS UNIFORM, BUT NOT BOILING. POUR INTO A COFFEE MUG AND THEN SPRINKLE WITH NUTMEG TO TASTE.

CLEANING
THE BATHROOM

Science has yet to determine the components of that strange stain behind the toilet seat, but all evidence points to substances that, when mixed, create something you wouldn't want to provoke or taunt in any way. Speaking of mixed, the Tub Scrubber offers a glassful of courage to deal with that stain and any other mildew, scum, and rogue hairs you may find when cleaning, even the ones with which you shouldn't mess.

THE TUB SCRUBBER

INGREDIENTS

2 OZ BRANDY
½ OZ SAUVIGNON BLANC
4 DASHES ANGOSTURA
   BITTERS

INSTRUCTIONS

COMBINE BRANDY, WINE, AND BITTERS IN A COCKTAIL SHAKER WITH ICE. STRAIN INTO A CHILLED COCKTAIL GLASS. MIXTURE CAN ALSO BE USED TO REMOVE MOLD FROM GROUT.

ORGANIZING
THE CLOSET

The closet is a chaotic jumble of clothes and loafers. Any visitor would see the disarray and ask how you made it through the earthquake. But the closet cop is bringing some order to this messy enclave and this officer is strapped with a whole bundle of new hangers and a shoe rack. Grandma's Hat Box is a classy companion to the dirty work, with a blend of soothing brandy and brisk sauvignon blanc.

GRANDMA'S HAT BOX

INGREDIENTS

2 OZ BRANDY
½ OZ SAUVIGNON BLANC
½ OZ CRÈME DE MENTHE

INSTRUCTIONS

MIX BRANDY, WINE, AND CRÈME DE MENTHE IN A COCKTAIL SHAKER WITH ICE. STRAIN INTO A CHILLED COCKTAIL GLASS. DECIDE TO KEEP THOSE JEANS YOU ALMOST FIT INTO BECAUSE THIS TIME YOU WILL LOSE THE WEIGHT.

MAKING
THE BED

There's just something wonderful about fresh sheets on a bed. Putting the fresh sheets on your bed, however, falls way short of wonderful. More physically and mentally exhausting than a gladiator tournament, you must contend with whipping waves of fabric as the sheets are unfurled, discovering the top sheet is upside down, and beating the pillows into the case. Thank goodness for the citrusy blend of the Three Sheets, which will ensure you don't care if the top sheet is upside down or even if it's clean.

THE THREE SHEETS

INGREDIENTS

2 OZ GIN
1 OZ DRY VERMOUTH
ORANGINA

INSTRUCTIONS

MIX GIN AND VERMOUTH IN A COCKTAIL SHAKER WITH ICE. STRAIN INTO COCKTAIL GLASS WITH ICE AND TOP OFF WITH ORANGINA. DRINK UNTIL YOU'RE NO LONGER UPSET THE FITTED SHEET KEEPS POPPING OFF THE CORNERS OF THE MATTRESS.

COUNTING
SHEEP

Whether due to stress or excitement or sheer wakefulness, trouble falling asleep is annoying. Worse, it often amplifies whatever emotion or thought is keeping sleep at bay. The age-old tactic of counting sheep could work, but why not add an extra dose of effectiveness in the form of Past Midnight? This soothing cocktail will warm your innards and turn those numbers into slurred syllables to quickly shepherd you to dreamland.

PAST MIDNIGHT

INGREDIENTS

1 OZ MILK
1 EGG
1 OZ APPLE BRANDY
1 OZ RUM
2 TSP SIMPLE SYRUP
CINNAMON STICK

INSTRUCTIONS

WARM THE MILK IN A SMALL POT. SEPARATE THE EGG YOLK AND EGG WHITE AND THEN BEAT EACH VIGOROUSLY. IN A MUG, POUR THE WHIPPED EGG YOLK AND WHITE, BRANDY, RUM, SIMPLE SYRUP, AND WARM MILK. STIR AND GARNISH WITH A CINNAMON STICK. DRINK UNTIL YOU PASS OUT.

CHAPTER THREE

IT'S

PERS

ONAL

EXERCISING

Exercise has many benefits. Studies show exercise helps maintain not just physical health, but also mental health. Well, a good Hammy Pull can also help with the mental part. The potent combination of liquor will give your mind a great workout as you ping from calling your ex to deciding to get the band back together. And thanks to the spiced rum and whiskey, you're sure to feel the burn.

THE HAMMY PULL

INGREDIENTS

2 OZ AMARETTO
2 OZ BLUE CURAÇAO
2 OZ SPICED RUM
1 OZ WHISKEY
1 TSP HONEY

INSTRUCTIONS

COMBINE AMARETTO, CURAÇAO, RUM, WHISKEY, AND HONEY IN A COCKTAIL SHAKER WITH ICE. STRAIN INTO A COCKTAIL GLASS. PREPARE A BUCKET OF WATER FOR THE NIGHT'S INEVITABLE REENACTMENT OF THAT ONE SCENE FROM *FLASHDANCE*.

SHOWERING
POST-WORKOUT

It's not a real workout unless you break a sweat and your sweat is so broken you don't think it'll ever get fixed. Bask in the satisfying glow of that killer workout, but keep in mind that the glow also comes with an aroma. You're ready to hit the shower, but don't forget to give your liver a bit of a cool-down as well. You'll be amazed at the smooth flavor of the Shower Pull and how the color of the drink pairs with the aging tile in your bathroom.

THE SHOWER PULL

INGREDIENTS

2 OZ AMARETTO
2 OZ CURAÇAO
2 OZ SPICED RUM
1 OZ RYE
1 TSP HONEY
ORANGE

INSTRUCTIONS

COMBINE AMARETTO, CURAÇAO, RUM, RYE, AND HONEY IN A COCKTAIL SHAKER WITH ICE. STRAIN INTO A COCKTAIL GLASS. SQUEEZE AN ORANGE WEDGE INTO THE DRINK AND THEN GARNISH WITH A FRESH WEDGE. AND, HEY, EYES UP HERE.

WHILE ON THE TOPIC OF BATHROOM DUTIES, DID YOU KNOW "BATHTUB GIN" IS A MISNOMER? CONTRARY TO THE 1982 MUSICAL FILM *ANNIE*, BATHTUB GIN WAS NOT MADE IN A BATHTUB. WATER WAS A KEY INGREDIENT IN ILLEGAL GIN MADE DURING PROHIBITION, BUT THE JARS USED TO FERMENT THE MIX WERE TOO TALL TO BE FILLED IN A STANDARD SINK. SO, THEY WERE COMMONLY FILLED FROM THE TUB FAUCET, HENCE THE NAME. NEVER UNDERESTIMATE THE DESIRE FOR A STIFF DRINK.

SHAVING
YOUR LEGS

All of the pants and shorts are in the laundry and only dresses remain. Time to plow the fuzzy thicket of hair below the knee in an effort to keep nicknames like "Lady Bigfoot" and "Gorilla in the Mist" from flying around the office. The Tequila Fuzz will ensure a smooth set of gams. And if you happen to nick yourself, the dash of crimson grenadine provides an empathetic touch.

THE TEQUILA FUZZ

INGREDIENTS

3 OZ TEQUILA
1 OZ LIME JUICE
1 EGG WHITE
GINGER ALE
1 OZ GRENADINE
LIME

INSTRUCTIONS

MIX TEQUILA, LIME JUICE, AND EGG WHITE IN A SHAKER WITH ICE. SHAKE, THEN STRAIN INTO A PINT GLASS FILLED WITH ICE. TOP OFF WITH GINGER ALE. ADD A SPLASH OF GRENADINE AND GARNISH WITH LIME WEDGE. IN THE EVENT OF A NICK, USE BAND-AIDS AS NEEDED.

TRIMMING
YOUR BEARD

Sculpting scruff takes all the patience of raising a bonsai tree. With each snip, the hair becomes a wiry haiku. Is that a shock of gray? Will the newly shaped jawline look thinning? If a beard is shaven in the woods, does the lumberjack make a sound? Have a pull from a Barber of Seville. With its dollop of whipped cream mimicking a freshly lathered mug of shaving cream, it will help you answer these and other woolly questions.

THE BARBER OF SEVILLE

INGREDIENTS

2 OZ GIN
½ OZ SHERRY
½ OZ LEMON JUICE
½ OZ ORANGE JUICE
1½ TBSP SIMPLE SYRUP
1 DOLLOP WHIPPED
  CREAM

INSTRUCTIONS

COMBINE GIN, SHERRY, LEMON JUICE, ORANGE JUICE, AND SIMPLE SYRUP IN A SHAKER WITH ICE. SHAKE, THEN STRAIN INTO A MARTINI GLASS. ADD A DOLLOP OF WHIPPED CREAM ON TOP. ACTUAL SHAVING CREAM SHOULD NOT BE USED IN PLACE OF WHIPPED CREAM BECAUSE IT TASTES AWFUL.

MANSCAPING

Perhaps the beard looks fine, but the eyebrows look like a macramé snake. Or maybe it's just a matter of leveling that forest of hair on your chest. If a cleanup is in order, try the Barber of Seville, but swap the gin for whiskey (and skip the sherry) for the Wax Job. It'll calm the nerves as you approach the painful follicle removal.

THE WAX JOB

INGREDIENTS

2 OZ WHISKEY
½ OZ LEMON JUICE
½ OZ ORANGE JUICE
1½ TBSP SIMPLE SYRUP
1 DOLLOP WHIPPED
  CREAM

INSTRUCTIONS

COMBINE WHISKEY, LEMON JUICE, ORANGE JUICE, AND SIMPLE SYRUP IN A SHAKER WITH ICE. SHAKE, THEN STRAIN INTO A MARTINI GLASS. ADD A DOLLOP OF WHIPPED CREAM ON TOP. IF YOU WANT TO QUICKLY QUELL THE TEARS POST-WAXING, HOWEVER, JUST DRINK THE WHISKEY NEAT.

GETTING
DRESSED

With housecoat hanging open, you survey the contents of your closet. It looks like a display in a museum highlighting questionable fashion from the previous decade. With no time (or money) for a shopping spree, you must make do with the dated options. Don't worry, the embarrassment you feel about your capri pants and houndstooth top will wear off after a Boxer Brief. Or three.

THE BOXER BRIEF

INGREDIENTS

1 OZ PUNT E MES
1 OZ LEMON JUICE
1 OZ LIME JUICE
2 OZ ORANGE JUICE
½ OZ COCONUT CREAM
1 TSP AMARETTO
1 TSP POMEGRANATE
   JUICE

INSTRUCTIONS

MIX PUNT E MES, LEMON JUICE, LIME JUICE, ORANGE JUICE, COCONUT CREAM, AMARETTO, AND POMEGRANATE JUICE IN A BLENDER WITH ICE. POUR INTO A CHILLED COCKTAIL GLASS. FOR A COASTER, USE THAT SOCK THAT DOESN'T HAVE A MATE.

CLIPPING
TOENAILS

Your toes are starting to look like those of a Palawan stink badger or perhaps a crypto-zoological creature, like a yeti. Hoist your feet high and get out the heavy-duty clippers because this job is going to take precision, poise, and a stiff drink. The Little Piggy pairs nicely with maintaining toe hygiene, thanks to its bold blend of musky and sweet tones. The potent mix might also help cure any athlete's foot you have going on.

THE LITTLE PIGGY

INGREDIENTS

2 OZ SCOTCH
2 OZ GINGER ALE
1 TSP HONEY
CARBONATED WATER
LEMON

INSTRUCTIONS

FILL A COLLINS GLASS WITH ICE, THEN ADD SCOTCH AND GINGER ALE. DRIZZLE HONEY INTO THE GLASS, TOP OFF WITH CARBONATED WATER, AND GARNISH WITH A TWIST OF LEMON. STAY ALERT FOR TOENAIL SHRAPNEL.

CLIPPING
FINGERNAILS

Like those special knives advertised on late-night infomercials, your fingernails could slice through a tin can and still be sharp enough to cut a tomato. Your fingernails are so long, you're starting to understand why Freddy Kruger never texts his buddies. Before you take a clipper to them, however, get yourself a Hangnail. Slicing the lemon with your claws means one less utensil to wash.

THE HANGNAIL

INGREDIENTS

2 OZ SCOTCH
2 OZ 7UP
1 TSP HONEY
CARBONATED WATER
LEMON

INSTRUCTIONS

FILL A COLLINS GLASS WITH ICE, THEN ADD SCOTCH AND 7UP. DRIZZLE HONEY INTO THE GLASS, TOP OFF WITH CARBONATED WATER, AND GARNISH WITH A TWIST OF LEMON. THOUGH PRACTICAL, DO NOT USE A NAIL FILE TO MIX THE DRINK.

CHAPTER FOUR

HOME

AND OTHER

OFFICE
XYMORONS

PAYING
BILLS

Cable, electric, water, gas, Internet, cellular, mortgage, *Cat Fancy* subscription—bills are due, so it's time to whittle away at your paycheck. The biggest challenge is trying to determine which bills need to be paid right away and which can wait a week or two. As you consider whether or not you could make it a month with no hot water, enjoy the Debt Charge. It cools your head and warms your soul.

THE DEBT CHARGE

INGREDIENTS

½ OZ VODKA
½ OZ BLUEBERRY
  SCHNAPPS
1 OZ WATERMELON
  SCHNAPPS
1 PINT BEER

INSTRUCTIONS

POUR VODKA AND SCHNAPPS INTO A SHOT GLASS. POUR BEER INTO A PINT GLASS. STOP WHEN THE GLASS IS ABOUT HALF FULL DROP THE SHOT INTO THE BEER. POUR OUT A SPLASH OF THE REMAINING BEER FOR YOUR LATE FEE.

THROWING AWAY
JUNK MAIL

Thanks to the rise of emails and digital bill payments, it's a fairly safe guess that anything coming to your physical mailbox is junk mail. Coupons for local restaurants, a postcard announcing a new dental office, some real estate flyers—nothing that couldn't be found online, but there's something quaint and old-timey about businesses and individuals who haven't discovered promoting with the ease of social media. As you transfer the unnecessary deliveries directly from the mailbox to the recycling, bend your other elbow and quaff a Valpak. That's an offer you can't turn down.

THE VALPAK

INGREDIENTS

6 OZ PINOT NOIR
½ OZ KIRSCHWASSER
½ OZ TRIPLE SEC
½ OZ HONEY
LEMON
CINNAMON STICK

INSTRUCTIONS

MIX WINE, KIRSCHWASSER, TRIPLE SEC, AND HONEY IN A SAUCEPAN. WARM OVER LOW HEAT. POUR HOT MIXTURE INTO A COFFEE MUG, THEN GARNISH WITH A LEMON WEDGE AND CINNAMON STICK. CONSIDER HAVING YOUR CAR DETAILED AT CENTRAL CAR WASH FOR JUST $20!

DOING
YOUR TAXES

The government wants your money, so it's time to dig out that sporadically maintained shoebox of receipts and see if there's a way to claim your shih tzu, Mr. Sparky, as a dependent. You can't afford the update to your tax software, so you dust off your calculator, which would roll its eyes if it could. Thankfully, you have the Sazertax to help you get creative with the deductions.

THE SAZERTAX

INGREDIENTS

ABSINTHE
3 DASHES PEYCHAUD'S
  BITTERS
2 DASHES ANGOSTURA
  BITTERS
1 TSP HONEY
2 OZ RYE
LEMON

INSTRUCTIONS

COAT THE INSIDE OF A ROCKS GLASS WITH ABSINTHE, THEN DUMP OUT THE EXCESS. POUR BITTERS AND HONEY INTO THE GLASS AND MIX. ADD THE RYE, FILL WITH ICE, AND THEN TWIST A LEMON PEEL OVER THE DRINK. SADLY, THERE IS NO LINE ITEM DEDUCTION FOR COCKTAILS.

WRITING
THANK-YOU NOTES

Birthdays and anniversaries are awful, right? Sure, presents are amazing, but why—dear God—why do you have to know so many generous people? You received a bunch of gifts and now you have to send a thank-you note to every considerate friend, family member, and acquaintance. Get the stationery and a fancy pen ready, but before you get started, pour yourself a Gratitudinal. The potent mix will quickly get you to that "I love you, man" stage, making the sentiments all the more convincing.

THE GRATITUDINAL

INGREDIENTS

2 OZ RUM
1 OZ BOURBON
1 OZ LEMON JUICE
¼ TSP PERNOD
4 DASHES PEYCHAUD'S
  BITTERS
CARBONATED WATER
ORANGE

INSTRUCTIONS

MIX RUM, BOURBON, LEMON JUICE, AND PERNOD IN A COCKTAIL SHAKER WITH ICE. STRAIN INTO A HIGHBALL GLASS FULL OF ICE. TOP OFF WITH CARBONATED WATER, ADD BITTERS, THEN GARNISH WITH AN ORANGE SLICE. IF THE NOTES ARE TO PEOPLE YOU DON'T LIKE, ADD AN EXTRA OUNCE OF RUM.

THE UNITED STATES OF AMERICA HAS
A NATIONAL BIRD (EAGLE), A NATIONAL
ANTHEM ("THE STAR-SPANGLED BANNER"),
A NATIONAL MOTTO (*E PLURIBUS UNUM*),
AND A NATIONAL FLOWER (ROSE), BUT
DID YOU KNOW THE COUNTRY ALSO HAS
A NATIONAL ALCOHOLIC DRINK (WELL,
KIND OF)? ACCORDING TO 2007's SENATE
RESOLUTION 294, THE LAND OF THE FREE
HAS RECOGNIZED ONE TYPE OF LIQUOR,
BOURBON, AS "AMERICA'S NATIVE SPIRIT,"
WHOSE GENESIS IS "INTERWOVEN WITH
THE HISTORY OF THE UNITED STATES." SO,
THE NEXT TIME YOU SIP ON A BOURBON,
CONSIDER YOURSELF A PATRIOT AND A
TRUE AMERICAN.

REFILLING
THE STAPLER

The stapler seems permanently locked shut. No matter how much pulling and pleading, the mechanism won't open and you have documents to combine. Before you start beating the device against the desk, take a few minutes and whip up a Swingline. The sweet citrus tang will revive your sense of determination to either open the wretched contraption or simply use a paper clip.

THE SWINGLINE

INGREDIENTS

PINEAPPLE
2 OZ TEQUILA
1 OZ ZINFANDEL GRAPE
  EAU DE VIE
1 OZ LIME JUICE
½ TSP AMARETTO

INSTRUCTIONS

CUT ONE-HALF OF THE PINEAPPLE INTO CHUNKS AND LIQUEFY IN A BLENDER. ADD TEQUILA, EAU DE VIE, LIME JUICE, AMARETTO, AND ICE. BLEND UNTIL SMOOTH. DOUBLE THE RECIPE AND DRINK FROM THE HOLLOWED-OUT PINEAPPLE. YOU CAN SHARE WITH A FRIEND—OR JUST SAVE YOURSELF A SECOND TRIP TO THE BLENDER.

ON THE TOPIC OF TEQUILA, THE STAPLE OF SPRING-BREAK DIETS EVERYWHERE HAS A GOD-LIKE PAST. PATECATL WAS THE AZTEC GOD OF A BUNCH OF THINGS, INCLUDING THE "ROOT OF THE PULQUE." PULQUE WAS AN EARLY FORM OF TEQUILA MADE FROM MAGUEY (WHICH IS A PLANT, NOT A POKÉMON). SIMILARLY, HIS WIFE, MAYAHUEL, WAS ALSO A GOD OF LOTS OF THINGS, ONE OF WHICH WAS MAGUEY. THINK OF THE TWO OF THEM AS YOUR MARRIED FRIENDS WHO ALWAYS LIKE TO PARTY…AND WHO HAVE SUPERPOWERS.

WRITING
A TO-DO LIST

There are a lot of things to get done and the best way to attack them all efficiently is to start with an organized list. It helps you order your thoughts, picture the various ways to accomplish each chore, and offers the divine satisfaction of crossing off items as you complete them. Yes, there's nothing more gratifying than a well-written to-do list, except perhaps the Priority One. The fizzy tonic will make sure you stay focused, stay refreshed, and stay happy. Of course, if "Restock the bar" is on your to-do list, you may have a bit of a conundrum.

THE PRIORITY ONE

INGREDIENTS

2 OZ TEQUILA
½ OZ CRÈME DE CASSIS
1 OZ ORANGE JUICE
1 OZ PINEAPPLE JUICE
7UP

INSTRUCTIONS

MIX TEQUILA, CRÈME DE CASSIS, ORANGE JUICE, AND PINEAPPLE JUICE IN A COCKTAIL SHAKER WITH ICE. STRAIN INTO A COLLINS GLASS, THEN TOP OFF WITH 7UP. ON YOUR LIST, CHECK OFF "MAKE MYSELF A GOOD DRINK."

SORTING
PHOTOS

Looking through old photographs requires a flawless gift for remembering details like dates, names, events, exactly which of your college roommate's suitors came to your junior year Halloween party dressed as a lobster. The #tbt pairs nicely with racking your brain to recall these and other details so you know how to categorize the images. Though if you already have a category called "Dudes Dressed as Lobsters," it will go faster.

#tbt

INGREDIENTS

2 OZ GIN
1 OZ SWEET VERMOUTH
1 DASH GRENADINE
1 EGG WHITE
MANGO

INSTRUCTIONS

MIX GIN, VERMOUTH, GRENADINE, AND EGG WHITE IN A COCKTAIL SHAKER WITH ICE. STRAIN INTO A COCKTAIL GLASS AND GARNISH WITH A SLICE OF MANGO. KEEP A MARKER HANDY FOR SCRIBBLING OVER THE FACES OF YOUR EX. (DO NOT DO THIS IF SORTING PHOTOS ON YOUR COMPUTER.)

ALPHABETIZING
YOUR COLLECTIONS

What is *The Godfather II* doing next to *The Catcher in the Rye* and why are they both stacked on top of *Mario Kart 7*? Books mixed with LPs, DVDs in the wrong cases—it's absolute anarchy! You need to get this stuff organized, stat. The spicy kick of a Librarian will keep you focused on what goes where and in what order. Before long, the shelves in your family room will rival the Library of Congress, minus the Dewey Decimal system.

THE LIBRARIAN

INGREDIENTS

2 OZ BRANDY
1 OZ SPICED RUM
½ TSP HONEY

INSTRUCTIONS

MIX BRANDY, RUM, AND HONEY IN A COCKTAIL SHAKER WITH ICE. STRAIN INTO A COCKTAIL GLASS. IF YOU'RE SAD BECAUSE YOUR ENTIRE COLLECTION OF ENTERTAINMENT OPTIONS IS STILL ANALOG, ADD TEARS TO TASTE.

SCHEDULING
A DOCTOR'S APPOINTMENT

Nearly a year has passed and thanks to countless organic salves, liquid cleanses, and Wiccan chants, you've managed to avoid needing to see your doctor for anything. But with more and more phantom pains and a cough that just won't quit, it's probably time for a checkup. Sip on a flavorful Copay while digging your insurance card out from the depths of your bag. It'll remind you of the delicious cough syrups of your childhood.

THE COPAY

INGREDIENTS

2 OZ SAUVIGNON BLANC
1 OZ BRANDY
½ OZ GRAND MARNIER
1 DASH ANGOSTURA
    BITTERS

INSTRUCTIONS

MIX WINE, BRANDY, AND GRAND MARNIER IN A COCKTAIL SHAKER WITH ICE. STRAIN INTO AN OLD FASHIONED GLASS WITH ICE. ADD BITTERS. DRINK TO BURN UP WHATEVER AILS YOU.

LET'S SAY YOU'RE A COWBOY OUT ON THE OPEN PLAINS, WHITTLING A NICE WOODEN PUPPY DOG FOR LITTLE JEREMIAH BACK ON THE HOMESTEAD. BUT THE KNIFE SLIPS AND GIVES YOU A GOOD SLICE ON YOUR PALM. LIKE ANY HARDENED RANGE RIDER, YOU'D REACH FOR YOUR BOTTLE OF WHISKEY AND DUMP SOME ON THE WOUND TO DISINFECT IT. SCIENCE SAYS THAT'S NOT THE SAFEST THING TO DO, ESPECIALLY IF YOU'RE THE TYPE OF COWBOY WHO PREFERS A NICE SYRAH RATHER THAN WHISKEY. IF YOU WANT A DRINK THAT ALSO EFFECTIVELY KILLS GERMS, THE BEST BET IS GRAIN ALCOHOL. GET ALONG, LITTLE DRUNKIE!

BEING ON HOLD
WITH THE CABLE COMPANY

The cable company's hold music loop has cycled by so many times now, you're actually starting to appreciate the artistry of the 1985 Casio SK-1 keyboard used to create the plinky renditions of your favorite songs. Hopefully, you'll be offered a home-appointment time frame that won't cause you to miss an entire day of work. Thankfully, the warming gin, playful vermouth, and energizing coffee of the Ten-Hour Window will give you plenty of sources to draw from to get through the call.

THE TEN-HOUR WINDOW

INGREDIENTS

2 OZ GIN
2 OZ SWEET VERMOUTH
1 OZ COLD COFFEE

INSTRUCTIONS

MIX GIN, VERMOUTH, AND COFFEE IN A BLENDER WITH ICE. POUR INTO CHILLED COCKTAIL GLASS. IF STARTING TO NOD OFF, ADD AN EXTRA SEVEN OR EIGHT SHOTS OF COFFEE.

CHAPTER FIVE

CYBER SPACED

OUT

UPDATING
YOUR OPERATING SYSTEM

Experts claimed everything would move and work efficiently in the future. Well, we're in the future now and your computer's software takes so long to update, it makes you long for the days of the abacus. Don't worry, the Commodore 64 is here to make the time fly by. The bite of the rye with a sweet citrus surprise will have you smiling even in the face of the Blue Screen of Death.

THE COMMODORE 64

INGREDIENTS

3 OZ RYE
½ OZ LEMON JUICE
½ OZ HONEY

INSTRUCTIONS

COMBINE RYE, LEMON JUICE, AND HONEY IN A COCKTAIL SHAKER WITH ICE. STRAIN INTO A CHILLED COCKTAIL GLASS. LET THE SLOW CRAWL OF THE UPDATE PROGRESS BAR LULL YOU INTO A TRANCE.

SPEAKING OF SCIENCE…WELL, *LOOSELY*
SPEAKING OF SCIENCE, OUR UNIVERSE
CONTAINS MIND-BOGGLING "ALCOHOL
CLOUDS." NEAR THE CONSTELLATION
AQUILA FLOATS A CLOUD OF HEATED ETHYL
ALCOHOL SO LARGE, IT COULD KEEP THE
ENTIRE POPULATION OF THE PLANET
EARTH BLACKOUT DRUNK FOR MORE THAN
A BILLION YEARS. OF COURSE, THE SPACE
BOOZE IS CURRENTLY MIXED WITH OTHER
ELEMENTS THAT WOULD KILL US ALL—AND
THAT'S ONE HANGOVER YOU DON'T WANT
TO EXPERIENCE.

RESETTING
A PASSWORD

Is it Pa55w0rd or maybe password123? Oh, wait! Is it p4sswor6? No. Hold on, is this the site that requires a non-alphanumeric symbol or is that Amazon? It looks like you'll have to go through the process of coming up with a totally new password again. It happens each time you visit the site, which isn't that often or you'd probably have an easier time remembering your login information. As you wait for the confirmation email, have a Mother's Maiden Name. The brandy and Kahlua will calm your nerves, while the milk calms your ulcer.

MOTHER'S MAIDEN NAME

INGREDIENTS

2 OZ BRANDY
1 OZ KAHLUA
1 OZ MILK

INSTRUCTIONS

MIX BRANDY, KAHLUA, AND MILK IN A COCKTAIL SHAKER WITH ICE. STRAIN INTO A COCKTAIL GLASS. DO NOT USE "KAHLUA" AS YOUR NEW PASSWORD BECAUSE YOU'LL FORGET HOW TO SPELL IT.

UNTANGLING
THE EARBUDS CABLE

Though you have no memory of fighting ninjas or falling down the side of a mountain, you assume that must have happened. That's the only way the earbuds in your pocket could have become so tangled. And the spastic snarl of wire is all that's keeping you from hearing your "Go Get 'Em" playlist, the one you use to get jazzed for a workout. With its jumble of whiskey, brandy, and fruit flavors, the Gordian Knot knows your pain.

THE GORDIAN KNOT

INGREDIENTS

2 OZ WHISKEY
½ OZ LIME JUICE
1 TSP RASPBERRY JUICE
1 TSP BRANDY
GINGER ALE
RASPBERRIES

INSTRUCTIONS

MIX WHISKEY, LIME JUICE, AND RASPBERRY JUICE IN A COCKTAIL SHAKER WITH ICE. STRAIN INTO A HIGHBALL GLASS, TOP OFF WITH GINGER ALE, AND THEN FLOAT THE BRANDY ON TOP. GARNISH WITH RASPBERRIES. IF YOUR HEADPHONES WON'T UNKNOT, LET YOUR MUSIC PLAYER DANGLE LIKE A MASSIVE EARRING.

MAKING
TRAVEL PLANS

Planning for the day when you can relax in a deck chair on a sunny beach and drink a delicious cocktail can take days, even weeks. So why wait for that cocktail? The Airfare couples perfectly with searching websites for great airline- or train-ticket deals as well as reading reviews of questionable hotels at your chosen destination.

THE AIRFARE

INGREDIENTS

2 OZ LIGHT RUM
½ OZ SWEET VERMOUTH
GINGER ALE
ORANGE
DRY ROASTED PEANUTS

INSTRUCTIONS

MIX RUM AND VERMOUTH IN A COCKTAIL SHAKER WITH ICE. STRAIN INTO A COCKTAIL GLASS AND ADD A SPLASH OF GINGER ALE. GARNISH WITH AN ORANGE WEDGE AND SERVE WITH A SMALL BOWL OF PEANUTS. A FEW OF THESE AND YOU'LL FEEL LIKE YOU'RE FLYING.

ANSWERING
EMAILS

In Vegas, big numbers are good. Also, big numbers are good in world records, paychecks, and most sports. They are not so good in your email inbox. Let's face it, once that message count passes five hundred, most people just succumb to the merciful black death of an email avalanche. But you are determined to dig your way out, one reply at a time. Good for you! You'll need a drink. The triple whammy of rum in the Reply All will get your fingers flying.

THE REPLY ALL

INGREDIENTS

2 OZ LIGHT RUM
2 OZ DARK RUM
½ OZ 151-PROOF RUM
2 OZ LIME JUICE
1 OZ MANGO JUICE
CARBONATED WATER
PINEAPPLE

INSTRUCTIONS

COMBINE LIGHT RUM, DARK RUM, 151 RUM, LIME JUICE, AND MANGO JUICE IN A COCKTAIL SHAKER WITH ICE. STRAIN INTO A COLLINS GLASS FILLED WITH ICE. TOP OFF WITH CARBONATED WATER AND GARNISH WITH A SLICE OF PINEAPPLE. IF THE EFFECTS OF THE DRINK TAKE TOO LONG, HIT YOURSELF IN THE HEAD WITH WHAT'S LEFT OF THE PINEAPPLE.

BY NO MEANS A SCIENTIFICALLY PROVEN FACT, A CITRUS SODA MIGHT BE THE MOST VERSATILE MIXER ANYONE COULD STOCK. WITH THE STAGGERING NUMBER OF COCKTAIL RECIPES THAT CALL FOR JUICES AND/OR ADDITIONAL SWEETENERS SUCH AS SIMPLE SYRUP OR BAR SUGAR, AN ORANGE OR LEMON SODA COVERS A LOT OF GROUND…OR RATHER IT COVERS A LOT OF LIQUID. PLUS, THE CARBONATION CAN DOUBLE FOR THE FIZZ USUALLY PROVIDED BY CLUB SODA, GINGER ALE, AND THEIR ILK. SO, KEEP A SIX-PACK OF CITRUS SODA AROUND AND CONSIDER YOUR BAR FULLY LOADED.

VIEWING
REAL ESTATE LISTINGS

Scanning realty sites is a lesson in managing expectations. Want a yard? How about a patio instead? Want a walkable neighborhood? Try one that's at least on a bus route. Maybe adjusting the price range or amenities will return more listings. Besides, what does an extra $10,000 really mean? (Aside from a steeper monthly mortgage rate.) The House Hunter is like a refreshing glass of lowered expectations.

THE HOUSE HUNTER

INGREDIENTS

2 OZ TEQUILA
1 OZ LIME JUICE
7UP
LIME
LEMON

INSTRUCTIONS

COMBINE THE TEQUILA AND LIME JUICE IN A COCKTAIL SHAKER WITH ICE. STRAIN INTO A COLLINS GLASS FILLED WITH ICE, TOP OFF WITH 7UP, STIR, AND THEN GARNISH WITH A LIME WEDGE AND A LEMON WEDGE. DO NOT, FOR A MINUTE, THINK THAT THE 7UP REPRESENTS A RISING MORTGAGE RATE. IT DOES, BUT DON'T THINK ABOUT IT.

UPDATING
YOUR RÉSUMÉ

When looking for a new job, it's critical that your résumé stun recipients. Sometimes, that means tweaking a few things, like your job title. (Hey, technically, a pizza delivery person is a Perishables Transportation Director.) You'll need to be thorough, honest, and creative. Mostly, creative. The Work History pairs nicely with padding experience, expanding your education, and coming up with elaborate reasons why each of your references is a buddy from college.

THE WORK HISTORY

INGREDIENTS

2 OZ WHISKEY
1 OZ GIN
1 OZ ABSINTHE

INSTRUCTIONS

MIX WHISKEY, GIN, AND ABSINTHE IN A COCKTAIL SHAKER WITH ICE, AND STRAIN INTO A COCKTAIL GLASS. MIXING THIS COCKTAIL DOES NOT COUNT AS PROFESSIONAL EXPERIENCE, BUT IT DOES COUNT AS A SPECIAL SKILL.

WISHING
SOMEONE HAPPY BIRTHDAY ONLINE

Facebook says it's your coworker's birthday, but you're getting the gift of a Birthday Candle. This potent shot has enough punch to make you actually care that Phyllis from accounting is turning forty-three-years-young today. Sure, you've only exchanged pleasantries with her in the breakroom a few times, but you don't want to look like a jerk. So throw back a Birthday Candle as you hunt for the perfect emoji that shows you acknowledge the cause for celebration without looking too overzealous.

THE BIRTHDAY CANDLE

INGREDIENTS

½ OZ KAHLUA
1½ OZ 151-PROOF RUM
LIGHTER

INSTRUCTIONS

POUR THE KAHLUA INTO A SHOT GLASS, THEN THE 151 RUM. LIGHT THE RUM ON FIRE. WISH THAT YOU'LL HAVE NO MORE BIRTHDAY NOTIFICATIONS IN YOUR FACEBOOK FEED. DON'T BLOW IT OUT, BUT RATHER LET THE FLAME BURN OUT *BEFORE* YOU DRINK.

CHAPTER SIX

THE NOT-

OUTD

SO - GREAT

OORS

WASHING
THE CAR

The car used to be Midnight Blue, now it's Road Dirt Beige. Even the "Wash Me" graffiti someone scrawled on the back window is barely legible under a blanket of fresh grime. Time to take hose and sponge to the trusty Corolla and remove the last four months of commuter dust and tree pollen. The Wax On will help limber up your elbows (and your attitude) to really get the suds working.

THE WAX ON

INGREDIENTS

3 OZ VODKA
½ OZ DRY VERMOUTH
1 OZ POMEGRANATE
   JUICE
STRAWBERRY

INSTRUCTIONS

MIX VODKA, VERMOUTH, AND POMEGRANATE JUICE IN A COCKTAIL SHAKER WITH ICE. STRAIN MIX INTO A COCKTAIL GLASS, THEN GARNISH WITH THE STRAWBERRY. PLACE THE DRINK FAR FROM LIQUID SOAP SO AS TO AVOID ACCIDENTALLY DRINKING THE CLEANSER.

CLEANING OUT
THE GARAGE

The garage serves as a sort of archeological site for your family's history. The shelves and walls are lined with dusty boxes bearing cryptic labels like "Living Room," "2003," and "Car Stuff." The Yard Sale is a sweet treat that offers a sugar rush to help you complete the task of selecting which things to keep and which to sell—all with enough booze to justify the decision to save that shoebox of hip-hop cassette tapes.

THE YARD SALE

INGREDIENTS

2 OZ VODKA
1 OZ KAHLUA
1 DASH PERNOD
VANILLA ICE CREAM
HERSHEY'S CHOCOLATE
  BAR

INSTRUCTIONS

MIX VODKA, KAHLUA, PERNOD, AND ICE CREAM IN A BLENDER. POUR INTO A WINE GLASS. BREAK OFF A SINGLE ROW OF SQUARES FROM THE CHOCOLATE BAR AND USE AS GARNISH. WALK DOWN MEMORY LANE AS YOU PERUSE THAT BOX OF BOOKS YOU HAVE KEPT SINCE ART SCHOOL.

COLLECTING
ITEMS TO DONATE

Maybe it's finally time to get rid of that set of encyclopedias from 1998 or perhaps someone else will find great joy in the slightly used surfboard leaning in a corner of the garage. Donating things to charity is a fantastic way to both help the community and help your sanity by clearing some space. And though you'll be sad to see that Easy-Bake Oven from your childhood go, sipping on a Goodwill Run fills you with a new kind of joy and the realization that you don't need to make cupcakes anymore because you have ice cream–based cocktails.

THE GOODWILL RUN

INGREDIENTS

2 OZ VODKA
1 OZ KAHLUA
1 DASH PERNOD
CHOCOLATE ICE CREAM

INSTRUCTIONS

MIX VODKA, KAHLUA, PERNOD, AND ICE CREAM IN A BLENDER. POUR INTO A WINE GLASS. FIGURE OUT HOW MUCH YOU CAN DEDUCT ON YOUR TAXES FOR DONATING THAT AWFUL LAMP AUNTIE DORIS GAVE YOU.

MOWING
THE LAWN

There's a beauty to the fact that people work hard so they can get a house with a lawn, which they must then work hard to cut every week. Pushing a mower back and forth across the yard has all the excitement of pacing with the added feature of physical exhaustion and, depending on the weather, possible heatstroke. The Grass Chopper won't make the job any easier, but after three of them, you won't care.

THE GRASS CHOPPER

INGREDIENTS

1 OZ CRÈME DE CACAO
1 OZ CRÈME DE MENTHE (GREEN)
1 OZ CREAM
DANDELION

INSTRUCTIONS

ADD CRÈME DE CACAO, CRÈME DE MENTHE, AND CREAM TO A COCKTAIL SHAKER WITH ICE. SHAKE, THEN STRAIN INTO A COCKTAIL GLASS. GARNISH WITH A DANDELION. FEEL FREE TO SUBSTITUTE ANY OTHER WEED FOR THE DANDELION, THOUGH POISON IVY IS PROBABLY A BAD CHOICE.

WATERING
PLANTS

Plants around the home and garden need a little refresher now and again, though water is recommended for them rather than cocktails. That's okay, however, because it just means more Plant Killer cocktail for you. This creamy libation is made from the juice of fruit trees you'd have in your yard if you were capable of keeping any plants alive.

THE PLANT KILLER

INGREDIENTS

2 OZ RUM
4 OZ PINEAPPLE JUICE
1 OZ ORANGE JUICE
1 OZ LEMON JUICE
1 OZ COCONUT CREAM
ORANGE
NUTMEG
GARDEN FLOWER

INSTRUCTIONS

FILL A SNIFTER GLASS WITH ICE, THEN POUR IN THE RUM, PINEAPPLE JUICE, ORANGE JUICE, LEMON JUICE, AND COCONUT CREAM. STIR WELL, THEN SPRINKLE NUTMEG ON TOP AND GARNISH WITH AN ORANGE WEDGE AND FLOWER. USE THE WATERING CAN TO HYDRATE BETWEEN DRINKS.

PULLING
WEEDS

Getting aggression out is healthy, but since randomly punching strangers is frowned upon, pulling weeds seems the next best violent method to vent that negative energy. It's not enough that you yank that goosegrass out, you need to make it feel awful in the process with a few choice insults about its mother. The Weed Killer's healthy dose of tequila aids in the chore by facilitating trash talk.

THE WEED KILLER

INGREDIENTS

2 OZ TEQUILA
4 OZ PINEAPPLE JUICE
1 OZ ORANGE JUICE
1 OZ LEMON JUICE
ORANGE
DANDELION

INSTRUCTIONS

FILL A SNIFTER GLASS WITH ICE, THEN POUR IN THE TEQUILA, PINEAPPLE JUICE, ORANGE JUICE, AND LEMON JUICE. STIR WELL, THEN GARNISH WITH AN ORANGE WEDGE AND DANDELION. CONSIDER LETTING YOUR LAWN "GO NATIVE."

TAKING OUT
THE TRASH

The trash can in the kitchen is so full, there's now a delicately constructed pile of empty containers and fruit rinds perched unsteadily on top, threatening to topple like a stinky avalanche. You must empty that can—*stat*. While carrying that putrid sack of waste away with one outstretched arm, quench your thirst with a delectable Two-Ply in your other hand. The balance between the trash and the cocktail gives new meaning to the phrase "waste not, want not."

THE TWO-PLY

INGREDIENTS

3 OZ BRANDY
½ OZ SWEET VERMOUTH
½ OZ LEMON JUICE
½ OZ APPLE JUICE
APRICOT

INSTRUCTIONS

MIX BRANDY, VERMOUTH, LEMON JUICE, AND APPLE JUICE IN A COCKTAIL SHAKER WITH ICE. STRAIN INTO A CHILLED COCKTAIL GLASS AND GARNISH WITH SLICE OF APRICOT. SHOVE ANOTHER APRICOT SLICE IN EACH NOSTRIL TO MASK THE SMELL OF GARBAGE.

SORTING
RECYCLABLES

Boxes and bottles and cans, oh my. In the pursuit of reducing your carbon footprint, you diligently put aside any waste that could possibly be recycled. Now you have a sizable collection of material that ensures the planet will live on for at least another week. As you put the aluminum in the blue bin and the glass in the green (or is it the other way around?), sip on a Milk Jug. The milk provides enough vitamin D and calcium to call it a healthy drink and the whiskey is your reward for keeping the planet healthy.

THE MILK JUG

INGREDIENTS

3 OZ WHISKEY
8 OZ WHOLE MILK
1 TSP HONEY
GARAM MASALA

INSTRUCTIONS

MIX WHISKEY, MILK, AND HONEY IN A COCKTAIL SHAKER WITH ICE. STRAIN INTO A COLLINS GLASS, THEN SPRINKLE GARAM MASALA ON TOP. DRINK AND REPEAT UNTIL WHISKEY BOTTLE AND MILK CONTAINER ARE EMPTY AND READY TO BE SORTED.

STACKING
FIREWOOD

A chill fills the air as the seasons change. Time to unpack the sweaters and scarves and start planning out exactly how to get revenge on the Wilson family down the street for last year's Thanksgiving Break Snowball Assault. No matter how things go down, you and your kin will surely be warm thanks to your deftly stacked firewood, purchased by you from the 7-Eleven in town. Have a Lumberjacked. You deserve it.

THE LUMBERJACKED

INGREDIENTS

2 OZ LIGHT RUM
1½ OZ LEMON JUICE
½ TSP BAR SUGAR
1 TBSP GRENADINE
CINNAMON STICK

INSTRUCTIONS

MIX RUM, LEMON JUICE, SUGAR, AND GRENADINE IN A COCKTAIL SHAKER WITH ICE. STRAIN MIXTURE INTO AN OLD FASHIONED GLASS AND THEN GARNISH WITH CINNAMON STICK. AFTER A FEW OF THESE, THE SPLINTERS WILL NO LONGER BOTHER YOU.

CHAPTER SEVEN

ALL I

FAM

N THE

ILY

CALLING
MOM

Is it better to receive guilt for not calling your mom or for some unknown offense only to be discovered when you call? Pour yourself a Subtle Insult and roll the dice. The frothy refreshment will soften any maternal blow—whether comparison to your sibling, fond memories of your ex, or the oft-asked "When are you going to give me some grandkids?"

THE SUBTLE INSULT

INGREDIENTS

2 OZ SLOE GIN
2 OZ ORANGE JUICE
1 OZ LEMON JUICE
1 EGG WHITE
CARBONATED WATER

INSTRUCTIONS

MIX SLOE GIN, ORANGE JUICE, LEMON JUICE, AND EGG WHITE IN A COCKTAIL SHAKER WITH ICE. STRAIN INTO A COLLINS GLASS FILLED WITH ICE. TOP OFF WITH CARBONATED WATER. DRINK AND REPEAT UNTIL YOU ARE WORTHY OF YOUR MOM'S SHAME.

TALKING
WITH THE IN-LAWS

Your partner's parents are in town and making themselves comfortable in the spare bedroom. There's no way to avoid them, so you might as well make yourself a Houseguest. This strong yet refreshing cocktail has a sweet flavor and bump of gin so you can fake a smile convincingly, even if the topic of your employment comes up and it's followed by the suggestion that you "just get a real job."

THE HOUSEGUEST

INGREDIENTS

2 OZ GIN
1 OZ LEMON JUICE
1 TSP GRENADINE
1 TSP HONEY
CLUB SODA

INSTRUCTIONS

MIX GIN, LEMON JUICE, GRENADINE, AND HONEY IN A COCKTAIL SHAKER WITH ICE. STRAIN INTO A HIGHBALL GLASS FILLED WITH ICE. TOP OFF WITH CLUB SODA. GARNISH WITH ANOTHER COCKTAIL BECAUSE THAT WILL BE ALL THAT GETS YOU THROUGH.

ALCOHOL ISN'T JUST FOR CELEBRATIONS. IT CAN ALSO BE A USEFUL AID FOR WARDING OFF MALARIA. BRITISH COLONISTS IN TROPICAL CLIMATES USED QUININE, A COMPONENT OF TONIC WATER, TO FIGHT OFF THE DISEASE SPREAD BY MOSQUITOES. BUT EVEN WITH ADDED SUGAR AND SODA, THE QUININE WAS BITTER, SO INGENIOUS BRITS ADDED GIN TO MAKE THE DRINK MORE PLEASANT. THUS, THE GIN & TONIC BECAME THE STAPLE DRINK OF THE ERA. SADLY, THOUGH THE CONCOCTION WILL KEEP THE BLOOD DISEASE AT BAY, IT WON'T DO ANYTHING TO SAVE YOU FROM UNWANTED COMPANY.

CHOOSING
A TV SHOW WITH YOUR SPOUSE

The day is done and you're ready for a little binge-watching. As your significant other snuggles next to you, the debate begins: Should you watch the new sci-fi series from that award-winning director or the elegant period drama from England? Oh, how about the docu-series about those grisly serial murders? As the conversation eats away at the TV time, sip on a Netflix and Chill. Its delicious fruity notes will make it okay that you both settle for watching *The West Wing* again.

THE NETFLIX AND CHILL

INGREDIENTS

2 OZ GIN
½ OZ CHERRY BRANDY
½ OZ CHARDONNAY
½ OZ LEMONADE
½ OZ CRÈME DE CASSIS
LEMON
POPCORN

INSTRUCTIONS

MIX GIN, BRANDY, WINE, LEMONADE, AND CRÈME DE CASSIS IN A COCKTAIL SHAKER WITH ICE. STRAIN INTO AN OLD FASHIONED GLASS. GARNISH WITH A SLICE OF LEMON IN THE GLASS AND A BOWL OF POPCORN OUT OF THE GLASS. IF DESIRED, RAISINETS CAN BE SUBSTITUTED FOR THE POPCORN.

LOTS OF COCKTAILS ARE MADE MORE MAGICAL BY CHEMISTRY. ONE SIMPLE EXPERIMENT YOU CAN DO IS A SHOT CALLED THE CEMENT MIXER. FILL ONE SHOT GLASS WITH BAILEY'S IRISH CREAM AND ANOTHER WITH LIME JUICE. POUR THE BAILEY'S INTO YOUR MOUTH, THEN THE LIME JUICE. THE CITRIC ACID IN THE JUICE IMMEDIATELY CURDLES THE CREAM CAUSING THE TWO LIQUIDS TO FORM A MUSHY SOLID THAT MUST BE CHEWED BEFORE SWALLOWING (THINK: ALCOHOLIC COTTAGE CHEESE). THIS ISN'T THE TYPE OF SCIENCE EXPERIMENT YOU SHOULD SHARE WITH YOUR KIDS UNTIL THEY'RE OLD ENOUGH TO CALL THEMSELVES A CAB HOME.

HELPING
YOUR CHILD WITH HOMEWORK

That bachelor's degree may have led to a nice job, but it doesn't seem to do any good when dealing with your child's homework. Seriously, what good is your education if you can't figure out one darn algebra equation? With the help of a refreshing Solve for X, you may not come to the right answers, but you'll undoubtedly come to *an* answer. And even if you're dead wrong on all of them, it's your kid getting the bad grade, not you.

SOLVE FOR X

INGREDIENTS

2 OZ BOURBON
1 OZ LEMONADE
3 OZ ORANGE JUICE
1 DASH SALT
LEMON

INSTRUCTIONS

MIX BOURBON, LEMONADE, ORANGE JUICE, AND SALT IN A COCKTAIL SHAKER WITH ICE. STRAIN INTO CHILLED SOUR GLASS AND GARNISH WITH A LEMON PEEL. DON'T LET YOUR CHILD SEE YOUR CALCULATOR.

WATCHING
A KIDS' SHOW WITH YOUR CHILD

They call this a plot? Clearly, the magic bunny is hiding in the flower patch. It's where the butterflies were going. If the turtle and his pal the tubby bear cub would just get their heads out of their...okay, calm down. It's just a kids' show. You are not the target audience, as evidenced by the repetitive music and volume at which the characters enthusiastically shout at the viewer. While your little one snuggles next to you on the couch, try a Barney's Revenge. It'll make this episode look like *Citizen Kane*.

BARNEY'S REVENGE

INGREDIENTS

1 OZ LIGHT RUM
½ OZ GIN
½ OZ BLENDED
   SCOTCH WHISKEY
½ OZ BLUE CURAÇAO
½ OZ CAMPARI
FINGER PUPPET

INSTRUCTIONS

MIX RUM, GIN, SCOTCH, CURAÇAO, AND CAMPARI IN A COCKTAIL SHAKER WITH ICE. POUR INTO AN OLD FASHIONED GLASS WITH ICE. GARNISH WITH A FINGER PUPPET. STARE INTO ITS SOULLESS EYES AS YOU DRINK.

EMPTYING
THE LITTER BOX

Mr. Binky happily rules his kingdom—from the kitchen to the spare bedroom. And Mr. Binky dutifully drops his dootie in his kingdom's official latrine. As a mere peasant, it falls to you to clean out this sandy receptacle. As you sift, Mr. Binky idles by, tail in the air to show you exactly what he thinks of you. You realize this is the only scenario in which the *lack* of opposable thumbs serves as an advantage. Otherwise, the furry little monarch could clean his own waste. Well, unlike your feline ruler, you can use those extra digits to prepare a potent Poo-Digger.

THE POO-DIGGER

INGREDIENTS

2 OZ RUM
½ OZ WHITE CURAÇAO
½ OZ PEACH SCHNAPPS
1 OZ LIME JUICE
BRAZIL NUT

INSTRUCTIONS

POUR RUM, CURAÇAO, SCHNAPPS, AND LIME JUICE INTO A COCKTAIL SHAKER WITH ICE. MIX, THEN POUR INTO AN OLD FASHIONED GLASS FILLED WITH ICE. ADD THE UNOPENED BRAZIL NUT AS A REMINDER OF EXACTLY WHAT YOU'RE DOING…BECAUSE IT LOOKS LIKE A POOP.

PLAYING
FETCH WITH THE DOG

There's nothing quite a pure as playing with your pup. Observe how magically the smell of the grass and fresh air blend with the boxcar-hobo odor of your mongrel. Yes, spending time with man's best friend can only be improved when joined by man's second-best friend—a drink. The Faulty Dog will have you wagging this cocktail all the way into your stomach.

THE FAULTY DOG

INGREDIENTS

SEA SALT
BAR SUGAR
ORANGE
2 OZ VODKA
GRAPEFRUIT JUICE

INSTRUCTIONS

MIX TOGETHER SALT AND SUGAR IN A SMALL SAUCER. USE A WEDGE OF ORANGE TO WET THE RIM OF AN OLD FASHIONED GLASS, THEN DIP THE RIM INTO THE SALT AND SUGAR BLEND. FILL GLASS WITH ICE, ADD VODKA, AND THEN TOP OFF WITH GRAPEFRUIT JUICE. ADD A NEW ORANGE WEDGE AS A GARNISH. REMEMBER WHICH HAND HOLDS THE BALL— YOU DON'T WANT TO TOSS YOUR DRINK ACROSS THE YARD.

CHAPTER EIGHT

OTHER

CRAP

READING
THE NEWSPAPER

The daily news is a great way to stay informed, break the ice at parties, or at least have a head start for when the apocalypse arrives. Of course, there are days when there's nothing but bad news. Even the most hardened wonk can sometimes find it a struggle not to crawl back into bed and wish away the stories. Though not technically a morning cocktail, Stop the Presses gives you the jolt you need to digest even the worst headlines over breakfast. Besides, any cocktail is a morning cocktail if you drink it before noon.

STOP THE PRESSES

INGREDIENTS

2 OZ GIN
1 TSP SWEET VERMOUTH
1 TSP DRY VERMOUTH
1 TSP LIME JUICE
1 TSP ORANGE JUICE
1 DASH ANGOSTURA
   BITTERS

INSTRUCTIONS

MIX GIN, SWEET AND DRY VERMOUTH, AND LIME AND ORANGE JUICES IN A SHAKER WITH ICE. STRAIN INTO A CHILLED COCKTAIL GLASS, THEN ADD BITTERS. DRINK THREE OF THESE BEFORE READING ANY STORIES ABOUT POLITICS.

READING
HEADLINES ONLINE

Remember when catching up with the news was an intimate affair? Just you and the newscaster—they'd tell you what was happening and you could consider it, then apply your own perspective. However, scanning online news is like an information mosh-pit. Headlines bait you to click, stories suppose "facts," and every article pleads with you to like or share or follow. The Stop the Madness helps quiet the din and eventually guide you to the only good thing on the Internet: cat gifs.

STOP THE MADNESS

INGREDIENTS

2 OZ GIN
2 TSP CHARDONNAY
1 TSP ORANGE JUICE
1 DASH ANGOSTURA
   BITTERS

INSTRUCTIONS

MIX GIN, WINE, AND ORANGE JUICE IN A SHAKER WITH ICE. STRAIN INTO A CHILLED COCKTAIL GLASS, THEN ADD BITTERS. WARNING: DRINKING THIS COCKTAIL MAY IMPAIR YOUR JUDGMENT ON WHAT POLITICAL STORIES TO SHARE ON FACEBOOK.

TAKING
A SELFIE

Your makeup is on point and your hair looks like you just walked out of the salon. Days like this are extremely rare, but you want everyone to think they're not. A selfie will show the world how good you are at life. (Never mind that from the waist down you're clad in dirty sweats and Crocs. It's all about creative cropping.) Before you snap the pic, sip on the #nofilter. It's a fruity blast of fun so sweet, you'll nearly have a diabetic seizure.

#nofilter

INGREDIENTS

2 OZ VODKA
1 OZ CRÈME DE CASSIS
1 OZ LEMONADE
GINGER ALE
RASPBERRIES
BLUEBERRIES

INSTRUCTIONS

POUR VODKA, CRÈME DE CASSIS, AND LEMONADE INTO A WINE GLASS FILLED WITH ICE. POUR IN GINGER ALE, LEAVING SOME ROOM AT THE TOP. STIR, THEN GARNISH WITH SMALL HANDFUL OF BERRIES. TAKE A PICTURE BEFORE YOU DRINK SO YOU CAN POST IT. #soblessed

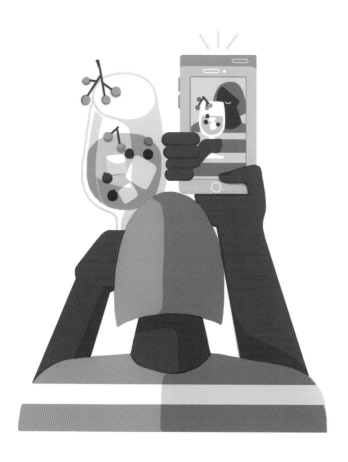

LOOKING
FOR CAR KEYS

The hooks by the front door are there for a reason! Why aren't the keys there? You'll never make it to the party (or movie or dinner date) in time. Might as well abort the mission. Still, you'll need to drive eventually, right? You have a job, after all. So, you set about mentally retracing your steps as you prepare to physically retrace them on a house-wide key hunt. Before you dive headfirst into the couch cushions, though, try a Plain Sight. The rich cocktail won't help you find your keys, but it ensures you won't care about canceling your plans.

THE PLAIN SIGHT

INGREDIENTS

2 OZ DARK RUM
1 TSP PERNOD
1 TSP COINTREAU
1 TSP KAHLUA
SUGAR CUBE

INSTRUCTIONS

MIX RUM, PERNOD, COINTREAU, AND KAHLUA IN A COCKTAIL SHAKER WITH ICE. DROP THE SUGAR CUBE INTO A SOUR GLASS, THEN STRAIN IN MIXTURE. STIR WITH YOUR CAR KEY—OH, HEY, YOU FOUND YOUR KEYS!

LOOKING
FOR EYEGLASSES

The night calls for a good round of binge-watching some classic television. Or maybe you'll try out that new streaming series, the one everyone's talking about. If only you could find your glasses so you don't have to keep your face inches from the screen just to see which character is speaking. As you clumsily meander from room to room hunting for your specs, sip on a 20/20. It's like a dessert you can drink. Plus, after a few, you'll realize it's just as entertaining to spend the evening binge-watching your cat.

THE 20/20

INGREDIENTS

2 OZ SPICED RUM
1 TSP PERNOD
1 TSP COINTREAU
1 TSP CHOCOLATE
    CREAM LIQUEUR

INSTRUCTIONS

MIX RUM, PERNOD, COINTREAU, AND CHOCOLATE CREAM LIQUEUR IN A COCKTAIL SHAKER WITH ICE. STRAIN INTO A SOUR GLASS. WARNING: TOO MANY OF THESE WILL DOUBLE YOUR VISION, MAKING YOUR GLASSES USELESS.

ASSEMBLING
IKEA FURNITURE

The instructions are right there and they look so easy and inviting, like a nice little cartoon about making an end table or dresser. Look at the illustrated people, look how much fun they're having. Though you've scanned the fun caricatures multiple times, where the heck you're supposed to put "peg C" eludes you, as does the exact location of "brackets 10-16," "panel H," and your partner who was supposed to be helping you. The Vad är Detta will help you make sense of those instructions, even if you end up with an art installation instead of a piece of furniture.

VAD ÄR DETTA

INGREDIENTS

2 OZ BOURBON
½ OZ DRY VERMOUTH
½ OZ LILLET ROUGE
1 DASH ANGOSTURA
   BITTERS
1 EGG WHITE
SUGAR CUBE

INSTRUCTIONS

MIX BOURBON, VERMOUTH, LILLET ROUGE, BITTERS, AND HALF OF THE EGG WHITE IN A COCKTAIL SHAKER WITH ICE. DROP THE SUGAR CUBE INTO AN OLD FASHIONED GLASS, THEN STRAIN THE MIXTURE OVER IT. STIR WITH AN ALLEN WRENCH—THERE'LL DEFINITELY BE ONE IN THE BOX.

HOOKING UP
A STEREO

Boom boxes were never this complicated. You just put in your Air Supply cassette and hit play. But hooking up a modern stereo is like defusing a bomb. Does the red wire go in the right or left output? And does the audio from the TV connect to jack number 5 or 6? While you pore over the tiny text in the incredibly detailed manual, sip on a flavorful Aux Input. Until you get the new system up and running, just put your mobile device into a plastic cup to amplify the music.

THE AUX INPUT

INGREDIENTS

2 OZ GIN
½ OZ LIGHT RUM
1 OZ LEMON JUICE
½ TSP BAR SUGAR
1 EGG WHITE

INSTRUCTIONS

MIX GIN, RUM, LEMON JUICE, SUGAR, AND HALF OF THE EGG WHITE IN A COCKTAIL SHAKER WITH ICE. STRAIN INTO A COCKTAIL GLASS. LISTEN TO THE SWEET MUSIC IT MAKES AS IT FILLS THE GLASS.

SETTING UP
YOUR HOME WI-FI

The cable guy could've set up your network, but you said you could handle it. Now, you're trying to figure out the difference between WPA and WPA2 security protocols and you don't have the benefit of a working wireless network to look it up online. Before you potentially open up access for your neighbors to peruse your entire digital music library and all of your tax records for the past five years, whip up a Router Input. It won't answer your questions, but after a few you'll confidently choose the answers, even if they're all wrong.

THE ROUTER INPUT

INGREDIENTS

2 OZ GIN
½ OZ DARK RUM
1 OZ LEMON JUICE
½ TSP HONEY
1 EGG WHITE

INSTRUCTIONS

MIX GIN, RUM, LEMON JUICE, HONEY, AND HALF OF THE EGG WHITE IN A COCKTAIL SHAKER WITH ICE. STRAIN INTO A COCKTAIL GLASS. DON'T LET THE DEVICE PICK A LAME NETWORK NAME, LIKE INNI-TECH ROUTER 37940287.

CHECKING
FIRE ALARM BATTERIES

Ah, the smoke detector's call, like that of a shrill and peppy robotic dog, can only save lives if the batteries have juice. To test that deafening shriek, you may need a cocktail. And nothing says "save my family from a three-alarm fire" like a good spicy Smoke Inhalation Mary. This spin on the Bloody Mary is not for the faint of heart. Hell, it's barely for human consumption.

THE SMOKE INHALATION MARY

INGREDIENTS

3 OZ VODKA
½ OZ LIME JUICE
½ OZ BARBECUE SAUCE
4 DASHES
    WORCESTERSHIRE
    SAUCE
2 DASHES HUY FONG
    SRIRACHA SAUCE
2 CLOVES GARLIC
TOMATO JUICE
GROUND PEPPER
JALAPEÑO PEPPER

INSTRUCTIONS

COMBINE VODKA, LIME JUICE, AND SAUCES IN A COCKTAIL SHAKER WITH ICE. MUDDLE THE GARLIC IN A PINT GLASS, THEN FILL WITH ICE. STRAIN MIXTURE INTO THE PINT GLASS. TOP OFF WITH TOMATO JUICE, SPRINKLE GROUND PEPPER TO TASTE, AND GARNISH WITH THE JALAPEÑO PEPPER. DIAL 91 ON YOUR CELL, SO WHEN YOUR MOUTH CATCHES FIRE AND YOU NEED TO CALL FOR HELP, YOU ONLY HAVE TO HIT 1.

CHANGING
A LIGHT BULB

The last tug on the lamp chain proved fatal. The brilliant flash, followed by darkness, signaled the death of the bulb. And though the new moody tone of the dim room could be a nice change, it seems impossible to blindly navigate around the low coffee table without suffering bumped shins or worse. On your way to grab a spare bulb, stop by the kitchen and whip up a Thomas Edison. Named for the man who gave us modern lighting, the bright taste of the cocktail will shine a light on any task and will even make a bumped shin feel better.

THE THOMAS EDISON

INGREDIENTS

1½ OZ WHISKEY
1½ OZ GIN
1 OZ LEMONADE
1 TSP GRENADINE
LEMON

INSTRUCTIONS

MIX WHISKEY, GIN, LEMONADE, AND GRENADINE IN A COCKTAIL SHAKER WITH ICE. STRAIN INTO A SOUR GLASS AND GARNISH WITH A LEMON WEDGE. IF REACHING THE LIGHT REQUIRES A LADDER, MAYBE HOLD OFF ON THE COCKTAIL UNTIL YOU'RE DONE.

PACKING
HOLIDAY DECORATIONS

Whether it's July 5th, November 1st, December 26th, or any of the other dates that follow major holidays, the thankless work of taking down decorations must be done. After all, you don't want to be the neighbor who throws away their Christmas tree at the start of spring break, do you? Break out the boxes, but before you swap out your patriotic lawn ornaments or wrestle the fake spider webs out of the hedges, make a Zombie Claus. And don't worry about the tangle of Christmas lights. You can deal with that next year.

THE ZOMBIE CLAUS

INGREDIENTS

3 OZ SAUVIGNON BLANC
2 OZ LIME JUICE
2 OZ ORANGE JUICE
2 OZ PINEAPPLE JUICE
2 OZ APPLE JUICE
1 OZ GRENADINE
½ OZ ALMOND SYRUP
MINT SPRIG

INSTRUCTIONS

MIX WINE, THE JUICES, GRENADINE, AND ALMOND SYRUP IN A BLENDER WITH ICE. POUR INTO A COCKTAIL GLASS AND GARNISH WITH MINT SPRIG. DO NOT ATTEMPT TO DRINK WHILE WEARING VAMPIRE TEETH.